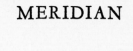

MERIDIAN

MERIDIAN

POEMS
1923 = 1932

By

BERNICE KENYON

Author of

SONGS OF UNREST

CHARLES SCRIBNER'S SONS

NEW YORK · LONDON

1933

156643

Foley

FOR
MY HUSBAND
WALTER GILKYSON

Many of these poems appeared first in *The Atlantic Monthly*, *The American Mercury*, The Conning Tower in the New York *World* and in the New York *Herald Tribune*, *The North American Review*, *The Outlook*, *Scribner's Magazine*, and *The Smart Set*. The author's thanks are due to the editors of these publications, for their courteous permission to reprint them here.

CONTENTS

PART ONE

FULL MOON

Two moons till harvest—why will you think of harvest?
The low strained branch—the broken frosted vine?
Here where we stand the meadow is white beyond us,
Here is the sweet divine
Fragrance of flowering linden. You can reap
No harvest from a linden, only the smell
Of heaven that drifts down so close around us . . .
And it is well
We cannot store that essence for our winter.
What should we do, my love, what should we do
Releasing into a distant winter midnight
A little of it—a few
Breaths of midsummer, hopelessly to taunt us,
There where we sit together in the cold—
There when we turn and face each other and tremble,
Finding that we are old?
No, in those days we shall comfort ourselves with apples,
With simple cakes fresh-baked in the ashes' glow—
Brown wheaten cakes from a far distant harvest;
And then we shall know
That all things run at last to a moonless darkness.
We shall forget, there in our winter gloom,
The green midsummer—the high moon riding whitely—
The linden all in bloom.

RETURN

Never return in August to what you love;
Along the leaves will be rust
And over the hedges dust,
And in the air vague thunder and silence burning . . .
Choose some happier time for your returning.

Choose spring, acrid and cool, unshaped, unmade;
See all that you love come awake,
Streams swell and buds break;
Or choose some autumn month with loud winds crying,
Stormy with leaves and dark birds southward flying.

Choose winter if you must, for that stark season
Waits, as you learned to wait,
For loveliness come late;
And all that you have longed for you may hold
Safely within the winter's barren cold.

But never return in summer to what you love . . .
O heavy beauty that my eyes possess,
O deepest beauty past its perfectness,
Where is the mad bright wonder, the divine
Rapturous lightness that eludes all sense—
That is like flame—that is like wind—like wine—
Only more strange and sweet of influence?
Where are you? Where?
The smell of fruit hangs in the windless air.

THE LETTER

"THEREFORE take comfort from this sheet of paper
On which your lover has written words of light;
And then destroy it—burn it at a taper
Held in a trembling hand, on a chill night."

Darkness shuts in—the night is cold—my fingers
Are cold too.   The cold clutches at my heart.
There is no mortal warmth at all that lingers
Here in your letter; and no skillful art

Has set the feeling of life down with the writing.
I am aware only of what you say—
And here you write forever of feasting and fighting—
And what are they, in this cold?—and what are they?

Nothing of you comes nearer for my reading . . .
Do you know what this night is like?—But you cannot know.
There are dark winds over the world; they are moving and speeding,
Forever bringing the cold; and they blow and blow,

Rattling my windows, shrilling the air, and sighing;
Making a sound of lost things in a storm—
Pursued things—hurt and wild—running and flying . . .
I will burn your letter up to get me warm!

Here is the candle . . . Never does flame mount quicker
Than in white paper, snapping, and turning it black;
The fire spurts—shrivels—dies in a final flicker . . .
And the cold—the terrible cold—comes creeping back.

SOMBRE SERENADE

Now since this night is only one breath long,
Now that the hour is late,
Open your window for a final song
Sung from the gathered shadow and the depth
Of silence where I wait.

You who have never waited, nor felt time
Stealing your anxious breath,
Look down, look down, before the clock's far chime
Strikes a last note, and our brief days run out,
And we are found by death.

For death is close upon the heels of those
Who love; and you will see
How fast he comes—how many ways he knows
To track my steps, or yours who will not once
Look down and answer me.

And soon the summer will be done, and soon
No one will sing for you
From the still poplar-shade, and no late moon
Silver the garden leaves, no lover at all
Tread dark on the bright dew.

And there will be but cold wind in this place,
A raw wind full of rain—
Singing the ageless night, but not your face;
Singing the dark, unmindful that you watch
Behind your window-pane.

AFTER MUSIC

In any room where songs were sung
Returning echoes mock the void
Of silence, stirring low among
Dark shadows of a peace destroyed:

Such peace as was not hard to bear
Before the singing had been heard;
Poor peace—poor silence—everywhere
By wandering echoes blown and stirred.

Oh sad am I, whose hollow brain,
And body empty now of song,
Resound to ghostly tunes, to vain
Vague echoes, day-long and night-long.

QUIET

Out of confusion, out of conflicting voices,
My song was woven. Forever in my head
The wild sounds were drawn together, and twisted
Into a moving music, a secret luminous thread
Which the mind followed, wanting a far ending—
Wanting a joy like silence. Now the bright strength
Of the song is done; I am done with all confusion;
The thread is spun to its length.

Because all worldly voices are remote and quiet
Since my ears at last are attuned to your repose,
Because you are near, I am happy to be done with singing;
I can sit languidly, and contemplate the rose
Bending upon its stem in the red of evening,
Unmoved by the twilight waning, by dusk in the air.
And the turmoil of the world, far and beyond knowing,
It is not for me now. I am silent. I am unaware.

NOT FOR LOVE ONLY

Not for love only,
But for the undefined
Varying brightness and shadow
Of your mood and your mind—
For your will or your yielding,
For all that you have or lack—
Though you drove me a thousand miles from you,
Yet would I come back.

Not for what you say on starry mornings,
Or dream about in white nights;
Not for all your gentleness,
Or the most profound and fierce delights;
But for our moments no more uncommon
Than our days of sun and rain—
Though you sent me away from you forever,
I should come back again.

And for love?—There is no describing
How I am held—how inescapably
The strong bond holds me now.   I can only tell you
That if one time you chance to see
Death in the doorway bidding me to follow—
Shaking his fist, shouting that I delay—
Even then—even then, my dear, if you are near me
I shall not go away.

DEPARTURE

I

THIS is the only house that I shall found
Ever again on earth. From now, beware!
What building I shall do will be in air,
Safe from the sands—cut off from lovely ground
That breeds too many wonders, and chokes me round
With high green walls of beauty and despair.
Now with the last strength in me I must dare
To leave this place, and forever be unbound.

Let us go free and find us wider room,
For it were death to stay too long inside.
Fling the door open, put the windows wide!
Let us go out before it is too late,
Past the long garden pale with fullest bloom,—
And never look behind nor lock the gate.

II

Now like a menace to the soul departing
From life itself, stands every plant and tree,
Fixed in a windless immobility.
The breathless crickets, and the lizards darting
Over the walls wait startled,—but they are staying
Here, by their stones, to forget us presently.
Our path drops down through meadows to the sea . . .
The birds poise, balanced, to jeer at us delaying.

Only the sky—the stormy grim expanse—
Bends to detain us, where across the north
Are built and unbuilt palaces and towers,
Dark leaden walls that bloom with a moment's flowers—
Shining to taunt us, flaunting impermanence—
A moment's brightness—only a moment's worth.

III

When we build again, our house shall be of cloud.
Till then, fix not your feet on any space;
Never put finger to the ground, nor trace
The outline of a garden, nor let the crowd
Of grass and myrtle and wintergreen, endowed
With too much fragrance, dampen your hands, and fill
Your body with lethargy. And never until
We forget this hour, stand still, or cry aloud.

You are no tree with long roots to be broken;
You are no plant to wilt in a wreck of leaves!
You are a being like the wind of the sky . . .
Cease to cry out, for he is a fool who grieves.
It is better to go with every grief unspoken,
And to choke the voice in your throat, if you must cry.

PREVAILING WINDS

I AM tired of describing—of saying words . . .
 Let the day fail—
Let the year run out—let the grim birds
Fly south . . . I will turn back into the winds again, after a while;
 They are the strong winds, and they prevail.

I am tired of trying to find where things begin and end,
 And of putting thoughts together;
But I shall keep on, as you know. I would only bend
My head for a moment against you, before I go out
 Into the world and into the furious weather.

No doubt right now there are ships ready, with their sails set,
 Waiting for the tide
To take them off to sea, to be struck and met
By the trade-winds, strong and sometimes perilous . . .
 Now, whitely on the swelling water they ride

Implacable. Well, I am implacable too.
 I shall go on once more.
There are the winds blowing—but there is you,
Against whom I can lean for a moment and rest,
 Till I set off on this same tide, as always before.

Do not smile, that I seem foolish in what I say . . .
 Do not move . . .
My dear, how can you tell where I am going, or how long I shall be away?
And how should you know that I wait, that I rest here against you
 Because I love?

PART TWO

SONNETS IN PROTEST

The Lady replies to the Poet who wishes to immortalize her in his verses

I. She Has Left Him

I am the cruel one you hope to keep
Imprisoned in your rhyme, long after death;
Denying me the little boon of sleep
When I shall tire of this my laughing breath
That is no breath of love, but the discreet
Swift dalliance of the elusive mind,
Daring to be forever wild and fleet,
Leaving all heavy certainties behind.

For being swift and light—for this offense—
You do me glory in a deathless prison,
Praising my beauty and your own immense
And lonely world, made void to the horizon,
Once the abode of rapture, till I chose
To leave you—for what reason no one knows.

II. She Does Not Love Him

Ladies who loved had often in their hearts
A curious fear of sure mortality
That should conceal at length their beauteous arts
And put at naught their true reality;
But I, who have not loved you, think it well
To cloud no future with a mock despair
Whose secret workings you aspire to tell
In words as changeful as the moving air.

And since I will not be to you the fine
Furious wonder, passionate and warm,
Or turn me sudden, like some tropic sign,
Into a silence rapt and brooding harm,—
Since changeless I remain, do not aspire
To brighten me in your eternal fire.

III. She Wishes for Oblivion

Believe me if you can: I have no taste
For homage paid to me in death's despite—
For small eternities that may not waste
To nothingness in some near future night—
For words that scorn my silence, and relate
Forgotten fairness and forgotten praise.
I will not wear your cherished love and hate,
Who might sleep dark beneath oblivious days.

I have no wish to last until such time
As men may turn and smile and be mistaken
Over the reasons for your careful rhyme
Whose meaning some new love may hope to waken;
Death like a gradual sea had better drown
My worth, than you to fix its small renown.

IV. She Is No Treasure to Be Hoarded

You that deny me what I most demand,
The resolute infinity of change
Under death's alchemy, could not expand
Such simpleness as mine into a range
Of living that is broader than this life,
Partaking of a multitude of others
In whom my restless being could run rife,
That here beneath your sorrow waits and smothers.

For you secrete me in your narrow measure—
Press me in sonnets—chain me up in rhyme—
Guarding me like some sweetly hoarded treasure
Held as your loved possession for all time;
You will not see me as I am, beyond
All capture in your thin illusion's bond.

V. She Feels Confined in His Verses

And I am wearied with your artistry,
And grown a trifle bitter . . . Here between
Your little words, I live an agony
Of half-amused disdainfulness, and screen
My twisted face with these my flying hands—
Deliberate for all their wanton motion—
Scheming at length to break your sweet commands
And slip the pretty bonds of your devotion.

Yet helpless—destined to a cramping cage,
Because you saw so little with your sight,
Took of so little, never tried to gauge
The wider mind, nor feel the wide delight
That might have filled you, had your blindness broken
Into perception of my thoughts unspoken.

VI. She Plans to Escape

This is the way I plan to make escape:
I shall be other than you think to find me,
So that your words preserve a different shape,
Gathering, in a mesh that could not bind me,
Some one you thought to know—set store upon—
Liked to enwrap in delicate renown—
Her perfect definition, slowly done
In careful verse, you ruthlessly set down.

She is, in all your amber, like a fly
Doomed to an end of fluttering, immured
In liquid lucence, so her baneful eye
Looks out unseeing, lasting, and assured.
She is, for all your care, as dead as stone;
Nothing you knew—all you have ever known!

VII. She Will Go Her Ways

Out in the dark where flying feet elude
Their own cast shadows, swift as driven leaves,
I shall escape from you, whose multitude
Of woven words speak me a man who grieves
Less for a love in bare reality
Than for some fine and thin-created fiction
Such as no woman is, nor longs to be,
Though for the lack she earn your malediction.

Write if you will, in each enduring phrase,
Of her whose cruelty has brought you sorrow;
But when the past devours a thousand days,
And you count treasure for the hundred morrows,
You will be baffled with a wordless rage
To find your captive vanished from your cage.

BALLERINA

Upon the point of a needle there might stand
A hundred angels, so the learned said—
　　　(*Step—pirouette—like this!*)
Or a thousand, with poised wing and beckoning hand,
Slim bright confusion of pale ecstasy,
Blazing of haloes round each lifted head!
　　　(*Turn so—and throw a kiss!*)

Where's their imagination?　Did the wise
Stay from the theatre?　Had they once seen me,
Or Mina yonder, needing a four-inch place
To point her toe on—wanting the whole stage
For any whirl the orchestra suggests—
Taking the centre—and she's twice my age—
(The unholy sight might well have hurt their eyes!)—
They would have known that the high joy of heaven,
And the celestial music that never rests,
Would scatter dancing angels to the seven
Circles of glory in the heights of Space!

Religion's too romantic, as dancers know.
Two make a stage as crowded as a hell;
　　　(*Leap—pirouette—like this!*)
So for their jealousy all dancers go
To hell, no doubt, and to a crowded doom
With needle-points to dance on—who can tell?
In heaven, praise God, they give the angels room!
　　　(*Pause so—and throw a kiss!*)

24

MEDIÆVAL

If you ask me why she is lovely, I shall answer:
It is because of the stately way she has of moving,
Making a stir of air that is sweet like the stir of arras—
Taking her lightly-measured steps with a regal bearing.

She is one that you cannot know by the face uplifted,
Nor by the flutter of hands above rich-patterned fabric;
She is a woman wearing a mask of delicate laughter—
She who is small and bright and calm in the ancient manner.

If you ask me what she has known, that a mask conceals her,
Checking the sting of tears and the motion of lips that tremble,
I shall say she is sad, and has been sad too often—
Making her proud and strange, who today has tears for no one.

Now there is none would dare disturb the mask she is wearing;
Let her alone—beware of a secret scorn beneath it;
Count it enough that she is lovely and small and slender,
Here where the light grows warm, as it falls and clings around her.

INTERVAL IN A GREEK DANCE

Your motion is like a voice trying to say
What no voice can,
Whose notes will suddenly waver and fall away.
Your steps that softly ran
Swifter than light, and free,
Have paused before an immanent mystery.

You do not bend to the earth—you do not fear,
But poise and wait,
As a voice gone silent before a truth half clear,
Towering vague and great.
The loosened folds of your gown
Stir no more, but like carven stone flow down.

All quietly toward you moves the little air
Of your caught breath.
The life that quickens and holds and keeps aware
Your body, is still as death;
Like the thought, living unheard,
That is deeply known, but cannot break into word.

LISSA IN THE GARDEN

Now the sun and rain I wear,
Lightly resolute
In the autumn-time to bear
No man knows what fruit;

No man knows if any at all
Shapes within this bloom,
Or if fragrant petal-fall
Marks its finished doom.

No man knows, nor wastes a word
Of his asking breath . . .
I wait silent, deeply stirred
Now, by life and death.

"A WOMAN LIKE A SHELL"

You are the worn sea-haunted shell
That lapping tongues of brine and sand
Have ravaged—once the citadel
Of a shy beast that loved the swell
Of water beating on the land.

Nothing could live within you now;
Your bones are chalk, your blood is drained.
Yet the fair shape will still allow
Echoes that tell your life, and how
And why the living substance waned.

Possession, now, to roving men—
Home-set, they listen long to hear
The old sea-roar and thunder, when
Your emptiness gives back again
The loud blood racing in the ear.

PART THREE

THIS APRIL

It would take so small a fire to burn me—
So little water to drown . . .
I wonder what intrepid forces turn me
Back to this dreadful town?

Here the lengthening winter broods and lingers;
No spring breaks here.
And I am sick with longing to see the grass's fingers
Pricking pale and clear;

To see for one brief day the sky unclouded,
To breathe clear meadowy breath . . .
Here is only the sound of footsteps, crowded,
Hollow, empty as death,

Over sealed pavements, over the wild seeds springing
In arid places apart—
Over the sound of terrible futile singing,
Secretly in my heart.

It would take so light a blow to sunder
Body and hopeless brain . . .
What can ever hold me now, I wonder,
Safe in this town again?

THE TOWN IN SUMMER

This is a weary city; spring
Never walks here. Green leaves are dead
Long before autumn, lingering
In dull bronze patterns lightly spread
Along the streets. We tread them down
On all the pavements of the town.

We pass beneath low branches, turn
To see each other's face, and sigh,
And watch the haze of summer burn
The listless air,—and long to cry
Against time's passing; and cling fast
To short vain hours that cannot last.

And men are always burning leaves
In dusty piles, as we burn days . . .
Spring is what love wants, that it grieves
Along these early shrouded ways;
Spring is what love needs—so it knows
No end, and cares not how it goes.

NIGHT OF RAIN

BETTER the empty sorrow in the dark,
The crying heart, the crying eyes that stare
Blindly till morning, than the bitter flare
Of rainy street-lights, threaded spark to spark
To lure me from this room in my distress,
Out where you pass—far out beyond my sight.
Better to grope in this small space of night
For sleep, or peace, or any nothingness.

You are not here, and you will not return;
And if you came—the door is shut and locked,
And sealed with pride, and barred across with pain;
And now it is for quiet that I yearn . . .
I should but lie and listen, if you knocked—
Rain in my heart, and at my window rain.

THE OLD MEN SPEAK TOGETHER

CARTHAGE is down, and the white sea-cities have vanished
Under the water, and Tiryns is laid waste
As low as Tyre; and the last man was banished
From grey Mycenæ long ago, and rests somewhere forgotten.

And Troy dug up is only the ghost of Troy
Nine times recalled and gone again and lost.
Bright miles of sand have risen and fallen to destroy
The cities of Egypt, made forever, and with difficulty forsaken.

And the fortress towns, the outposts of the plain,
Are buried deep in grass; and fifty years
Blow over them like an hour; and soon in vain
You will search a thousand leagues of grass and never come upon them.

And my own city . . . and yours. . . . The streets ablaze,
The walls that were our good security,
The burning towers at which we used to gaze,
With all their windows shining infinitely—
Are they not dim already, and worn, and the colors faded?

SKY MEADOWS

THE great still meadows of the sky
Seem full of peace, when love's distress
Strikes at our hearts like music heard
From distances as limitless
As dream; and all entranced we lie
Gazing at cloud and bird.

From this remote and silent field
Our drowsy sight may lift and reach
Into the higher range of air;
And our vain thoughts, bent each to each,
May find it very sweet to yield
Their constant yearnings there.

Our small cupped valley holds the sun
Brimmed to its edges, meadow-deep
In goldenrod and fading clover . . .
Nothing abroad shall break our sleep,
Though leagues above, and one by one,
The southward geese fly over.

LAKE OF DROWNED TORCHES

(In the North Woods)

Whatever rivers enter here
To fill each gloomy dim lagoon
Will find no more that banks are clear
Or courses open to the moon.

Reaching their crystal fingers in,
They meet this shrouded, stiller land—
A lonely lurking-place to win
From their high course through shale and sand.

All roots of lilies and of cress—
The pungent weeds that waters hold—
Clasp through a sedgy wilderness;
And anchored in the blackest mold

They lift, through choking silt and mud,
Up to the surface of the air,
The heavy leaf and armored bud
That rest so clean and lightly there;

And lilies, opened to the dark,
Set luminously all about
And cupped to hold a greenish spark,
Are ghosts of torches long gone out.

GOURDON

If you but tossed a pebble over
The crags and cliffs toward the Loup River,
The chasms and slopes of the Loup River,
From this small eyrie rimmed with cloud,
I am sure the rocks would speak aloud—
Like sudden voices by creation
Startled into reverberation
Louder than all winds that sing
Along these heights.   The dropping sound,
The pebble falling from ledge to ledge,
Would suddenly and strangely ring;
Till birds in Mediterranean sedge
Great leagues away—long streaming miles—
Out on the far and level ground
Where water fringes the purple shore—
Would lift at the sound, wide wing by wing,
And cut across the cloudy aisles
And infinite tides of air once more.

If you should toss a pebble over,
This would happen . . . If you should say
One word into this silence, then
All the far cliffs cut by the river,
The crags that tower to the sky,
And all earth sensed and seen of men,
And you and I,
Would crumble at the terrible sound—
Break into sifted sand and air—
Fallen to atoms everywhere,
The wind would blow us over the ground!

AUTUMN FRAGMENT

It was the walnut trees that faded soonest,
Letting the autumn wind blow bare their branches,
Scattering speckled leaves in the golden thickets,
Empty and grey when the sumac turned to crimson.
    The chestnut trees shed all their fruit one night;
The hickory detached its leaflets, slid
Its glory into the dust.   The copse blew thin,
Smelling of frosty grapes and acrid berries.
    Small birds chattered together but never sang;
A lone crow stalked his field.   The bittersweet
Ran in the woods in mockery of faint green
Like a pale ghost of spring.   Wild asters withered.
Bronze and red and violet colors of oak
Stood a while like beaten metal burning
In the blue air, and on their night, burned out.
    It was the willow trees that faded latest;
Tipping the silver sides of their leaves from the wind,
They trembled, bearing up a cloudy green.
A long, long while they stood; and the frost found them.

MOCKING-BIRD IN AUTUMN

I HEAR you singing the robin, and I smell
The damp spring earth, the crocus lightly spread
In new green grass.   Perhaps the leaves are showing
On the bare bough.   I dream that overhead
Fair clouds ride high in fair winds gently blowing.

On this warm earth I lie and listen and dream,
Loving the land from which all life shall rise
Here in the sun . . . For how can I remember,
Resting here quietly, with my closed eyes,
That we are not in April, but September?

Singing the jay, you jeer at me and ask
Whatever I mean by doubting of your word . . .
Singing the wren, you would prove your season—singing
The wood-thrush for a promise—the oven-bird
For reassuring—the oriole's cry—the ringing

Voices of half a score of birds—while I
Might never know, for all your clamoring,
How near the year has come to bitter weather,
As you run on, voice after voice, and sing
All these fair empty promises together!

SOUTH

Oh now let autumn come as it must come—
It cannot redden the privet and the pine,
It cannot set the tall plane-trees to burning,
Nor gild the honeysuckle and trumpet-vine.

It cannot darken the grapes, that will stay green
Until they fall; and even the intense
High maples will have no blaze of glory upon them,
But wait in vain for their magnificence.

They will shed their thin leaves quietly, one at a time,
Dropping and falling and dropping to the sand . . .
Oh now let autumn come as it must come,
In mist and stillness waiting over the land;

In mist and cloud, and storms that shudder in darkness,
Bright without thunder, in the silence lost
Across the land where no stars will be rising
Till the whole world is empty and sharp with frost.

SOUTHERN WINTER

Do not follow me here—there is no sun,
Nor warmth for flowers trying bravely to bloom,
Nor any lightness for the heart, nor one
Moment of peace . . . There is, for dreams, no room.

The rushing terrible sea is hard as steel;
The clouds make silent tumult thwarting the light.
Do not follow me here, or you will feel
Heavy of heart by day, and lonely at night.

If mornings ever were blue in this queer land,
Or any softness gathered in the grey
Of evening light along the cold pale sand,
I should not tell you then to stay away.

But do not follow me here. The dark waves rise
To long recurrent thunder, heavy and slow.
Near you, in this bleak land where all hope dies,
I should be more alone than I am now.

PART FOUR

CAT'S WORLD

If I come in, you must leave the door ajar,
The window open, all the curtains parted
Showing the world outside . . . I am not faint-hearted;
You must not blame me. Only—where you are,
Locked to yourselves, shades drawn and air shut out,
I should feel restless, thinking there is no more
Beyond your walls—beyond your towering door!
I should feel lost, and cry, and walk about
Distractedly; remembering—not quite sure—
Thinking of strong cold wind, and winter trees,
And black fields frosted where I ran in fear
With night to shield me, endless—dim—secure;
Feeling uncertain in your warmth and ease . . .
I have come in, but do not hold me here!

TWO CATS ON THE HEARTH

REST quietly—the world moves toward its end . . .
Lie here content in warmth and gentleness;
Beyond the door the alien world's distress
Is well locked out, and the grim woods extend
Toward secret darkness where the plants shall bend
For other steps than ours, and their impress
Lasts but a moment.   Better this hearth, to bless
Our long repose, which men themselves defend.

The fire flows softly toward the yielding air—
There is a smooth dark stone beneath my head—
Time rolls away, forever unaware
Of you and me—waiting apart, instead,
The pleasure of our master, in his chair
Sitting and sleeping like the sculptured dead.

SONNETS WRITTEN IN THE PENNSYLVANIA STATION

I. CROWD

THEY are as numerous and separate
As sand—a light confusion, grain by grain
Disturbed and spread about and gathered again
And then sent sprawling, little specks and great,
As if there were no pattern in their fate.
Their myriad faces, hard and flat and plain,
Show, in a many-moleculed disdain,
Bright surfaces of splintery quartz and slate.

They do not live. There is not one is warm.
There is not one who cares to give or yield
An atom's breadth. They rasp against each other
Like the sharp flinty sand of a poor field.
You move among them only to your harm:
Resisting you, they prick and cut and smother.

II. Exits

You can find as many exits from this station
As there are ways to venture out of being,—
All of them dark, lest any mortal, seeing
The gloomy route, should dread the destination.
Bright names and loud resounding words alone
Set forth the kind of land a man may find
Beyond the gate where, confident and blind,
He takes his train and leaves for the unknown.

It would be good to hear where we are going—
Good to be certain, by a lovely mark,
A gleaming name with magic in the knowing,
Starred over every exit through the dark;
Then we might choose a gate, and say farewell,
And reach at will a heaven or a hell.

RADIO

I. Broadcast

Broadcast along the infinite seas of night,
How should our fragile music ever contrive
To hold its form and motion, and stay alive
Down the long currents where the stars have flight?
Fragments of order—the intensity
Of human voices—the light blare of brass,
And whispering cry of violins, must pass
In man's design, across immensity.

How far along the windy rapture of space,
How long upon the varying wastes of time
Our music moves, no one of us shall know.
We gather it up again and give it place
In some small room, to hear it roar and chime
With starry sounds and the night's black undertow.

II. Static

UNDER our music—over it—wave on wave
The great dark seas resound, and will be heard
Thundering down the night, until no word
Remains of earthly making.   All our brave
And momentary songs are torn asunder,
Ravelled and spun apart to the last trace;
Down the invisible tide of time and space
They are borne away, and the seas have dragged them under.

Thus is our order, pattern and design,
No more than cobweb—no more permanent
Than smoke flung far, than dreams burnt out and banished . . .
Thus is our music, intricate and fine
And lightly made, forever vainly sent
To ride the storms in which high stars have vanished.

SONNETS OF THE SANDHILLS

(*North Carolina*)

I. TWO GIRLS

Two tall black daughters of the sons of slaves
Wait in the broken shadow of a pine;
Beside the road they sit and give no sign.
The heat moves by them in translucent waves;
Behind them over the field once more the corn
Lifts shining leaves, bent by the wild pea vine;
The crows fly over in a wavering line—
It was the same—the same since they were born.
One digs her prim shoes idly in the sand,
Musing that nothing happens any more;
The other, languid, leans upon the ground
And gathers twigs and pebbles in her hand . . .
Filled with vague shadows of forgotten lore,
In the long noon they wait, and make no sound.

II. PEACH ORCHARD

"Next year," he said, "we'll cut these peach trees down.
Our good ones weren't so pretty when they bloomed;
These may be nice to look at, but they're doomed.
We've vowed next year they'll go."   I saw his frown,
No more than a frown, for this miraculous land—
Twelve thousand acres, spreading far and even,
The rosy pavement for the floor of heaven,
Checkered across the yellow slopes of sand.
Let us walk between the peach trees—bend the boughs
Down close around us, shake the petals free
In waves of color, sparkling waves of light,—
Take all our being can hold of this brief sight,
And then escape, and never come back to see
If farmers in the Sandhills keep their vows.

III. GREAT HEAT

THE air is full of thunder.   Miles away
Off to the south I hear the great drums beating
Continuously, their heavy strokes repeating
My own hard pulses through the blazing day.
On the flagged path, and on the brown burnt grass,
Our pine trees print a thin and meagre shade.
I wait in the drowsy house.   I am afraid
Of the bitter world and the even sky of brass.
In time the drums will be silent, when the light
Fades redly out across this sandy waste;
Then in the breathless air, all vague and dim,
But never dark—in the unreal white night
I shall go down to the pool, and at its brim
Drink the black water, silver to the taste.

IV. GRASS

Deep waves of grass curve downward in the sun,
Heavy with timothy and blooming clover . . .
We are not there to lie in them, my lover,
Nor count the birds that vanish one by one
Into the curve of sky above our head,
Nor hear the lonely notes of the quail and plover
Calling to silence, as the sun goes over,
Bringing the night too soon.   I know this dead
And sandy stubble, pricking at our knees,
Straggling across the blackened stumps of trees,
Is grass of a sort—the poor stuff of the south,
That dries and breaks and never learns to bend . . .
Lean close beside me in this time of drouth,
And let us hope the day is soon to end.

V. EVENING

I KNOW what you desire and cannot find:
Your eyes move over the lowland, wanting the sea.
One time at this cliff's foot monotonously
The warm bright water broke, where now, resigned,
Grimly the farmers plant a blistering field,
And never dare to hope for a rain at dawn.
This is the land where tide and forest withdrawn
Left only level sand that will not yield.
Now in late twilight when the mist once more
Covers the country, all the plain grows blue,
And at our feet the very ancient shore
Sounds with a myriad ripples, and the air
Blows salt, until you know the sea is there,
Where the blue dark spreads out to comfort you.

PART FIVE

MOMENT

On the still earth all deep in grass I lie
To watch blue heaven moving bright with cloud,
Turning beyond the thought of such as I
Who, with no timeless infinite endowed,
Would dream far boundaries for unbounded space
And minutes' order for this moving time,
When, on a day of gold, in this gold place
I watch the sky, and hear the noon hour chime.

Over my head, oblivious and intent,
The bees spin by toward higher fields than these;
A thrush's chant, poured out and softly spent,
Fades through dim thickets of the alder trees;
So swift the flight—so slow the lone bird's song—
I cannot tell if noon be short or long.

TIME

WELL then, since we are not secure but live
Forever in change, in patterns half-revealed,
Turned with the circling stars, swung out and wheeled
In dim designs whereof no positive
Limits are known—since only this is sure
For all our tense discovering, let us rest,
And fix our eyes upon the fading west,
And dream this darkening moment may endure.

Imagine that no hour can ever rise
Beyond our own, wherein the still embrace
Of twilight gathers, and the heavy skies
Blacken and drown the light of every place . . .
Dream that for all our change we never grow wise
To doubt this finite time in infinite space.

GREY NIGHT

ALL night, intrepid, tireless and serene,
I walk the earth and all the worlds beside;
All night the folded darkness opens wide
To let me pass unhurt and step between
The balanced orbits, toward the vaguely seen
And nebulous streamings of the starry tide—
Discovering the unknown, and the allied
Unknowable, and all that may have been.

All night, closed in and gratified by sleep,
My body waits, and cares not to restrain
Its wayward being off upon the deep
And timeless glimmerings where space runs out—
Content to wait till day, and once again
Dim my discoveries in the light of doubt.

FOR SLEEP

THERE is no way with sleep but to die each night—
Drop like a drowning swimmer in the flow
Of heavy waters crushing out the light,
Closing above a last thin watery glow.

Unfearing and unhoping, you must ride
The lonely current of a nameless stream
That bears you onward toward its ocean's tide
With weight of waters heavier than dream;

And down beyond the world at last you will sink
Deeper than time, and where all time is vain;
And in the abode of sleep, as beyond the brink
Of death, give up the body and the brain;

Knowing you cannot wake, nor any sound
Trouble your silence like a distant bell;
Knowing that nothingness will close you round,
And in its still embrace you will fare well.

EAST WIND

FROM this high place, the bare slope reaches out
To lower fields, but here the wind blows keen;
We brace our feet in the pliant frost-freed grass;
We stare, with the sunlight glittering in our eyes.
Wind—wind to lean against—sharp morning wind—
East wind that races through a vacant sky!
Here life mounts in the air—here life is rung
Like bells, in sunshine, to blue distances.

No hour could ever move us more with beauty . . .
Summer will deepen the shadows of all things,
There will be storms from the far line of hills;
But one loud song keeps running in my heart:
Glorious of all things—glorious forever—
The day of wind, the sky, and you who stand
Apart from me, yet near—and this worn grass
Whose thin grey blades are speared with newer green,—
And all the world spread out in the rising day—
Glorious of all things—glorious forever!

THE SWALLOWS

Down through the long air of summer the swallows glide,
And deep in the alders the wood-thrush goes on singing—his notes slide
Out from among the leaves.   Under a straight sun the world lies wide.

Summer is made of desire and space and passionate sweet sound.
Lie in the shade of the alders—press yourself to the grass, to the ground,
And watch the swallows flying and the pale motes of sun falling around.
Listen only a little to the thrush's notes, faintly shaken.
Watch how the swallows move—their swift trails will not again be taken.

Who but you will ever mark this bird's track through the golden sky?
He flashes away—through the pale air he flaunts and plunges by.
The thrush may repeat his song, but the trail of the swallow's flight
Closes and vanishes utterly.

OLD AGE

WHEN I am old I shall sit quietly
With folded hands, under the noonday sun;
And never let the past drift back to me,
And never hope for years not yet begun;

But watch, as I do today, ants in the grass,
And spiders patiently renewing webs,
And the unweary flight of gulls that pass
Along the river while the slow tide ebbs;

And see how bees take honey and wing out
In perilous winds, back to their secret hive;
And watch the flowers opening all about,
And clouds of gnats that dance to be alive;

Until I find myself grown less than these,
Heedless as they, and happy, at high noon,
Where, all unmindful of grim mysteries,
I can forget that death must take me soon.

PERIPETEIA

In the summer night it is good to lie
On a shelf of rock, with a warm stone pillow,
Heated through when the sun was high,
Washed by old rains, and weathered mellow,
Hollowed a little but not too deep,
Hard to the bones, but strong for sleep.

Some may seek a softer bed
But I like stone beneath my head,
Stone that was shaped dim years ago
Under a glacier's grinding flow,
Smooth to the cheek and warm and sound,
Firmer than grass and yielding ground.

Hours long in the summer night
The sky flows, and the river flows,
And the murmuring leaves of the trees are bright
And flowing with moonlight, never still;
The leaves grow out as the night grows—
The trees mount tall and the rock-plants spread—
I like still stone beneath my head!
Stone that stands at the crest of a hill,
Whose length is certain beyond increase,
That cannot stir as the grasses will,
But is moveless and high and full of peace.

For who shall rest who feels in his sleep
How all things change beyond recall?
That grass can thicken and hide him deep—
On a single night the wheat grow tall—
Above him branches cover the air—
The night-flowers open one by one—
Under his head the quick roots run—
How shall he sleep, then, unaware?

But on stone, hours without number,
Quiet and dreamless I would lie,
One lone dark thing deep in slumber,
Heedless of change as time flows by;
Letting the still rock hold and keep
This known place in the long unknown
Of the summer night, when, heavy with sleep
I drop to rest on my smooth stone.